Bierstadt

Bierstadt

By Gordon Hendricks

An essay and catalogue to accompany a retrospective exhibition of
the work of Albert Bierstadt

Presented at:

Amon Carter Museum, Fort Worth, Texas
January 27 — March 19, 1972

Corcoran Gallery of Art, Washington, D. C.
April 2 — May 14, 1972

The Whaling Museum, New Bedford, Massachusetts
May 28 — July 5, 1972

Whitney Museum of American Art, New York, New York
September 11 — November 5, 1972

Pennsylvania Academy of the Fine Arts, Philadelphia, Pennsylvania
November 15, 1972 — January 3, 1973

AMON CARTER MUSEUM, FORT WORTH

AMON CARTER MUSEUM OF WESTERN ART

BOARD OF TRUSTEES

The Amon Carter Museum was established in 1961 under the will of the late Amon G. Carter for the study and documentation of westering North America. The program of the Museum, expressed in publications, exhibitions, and permanent collections, reflects many aspects of American culture, both historic and contemporary.

ACKNOWLEDGMENTS

Of the romantic landscapists of the late nineteenth century, few are more closely identified with the American scene than Albert Bierstadt. His tremendous production, combined with extensive travel in this country, provide a vast reference of the artist's response to the spectacle of nature in America, especially western America. It is strange, then, that the artist's work has only once before been assembled in anything like a representative exhibition (Santa Barbara Museum of Art, 1964).

On the chance there is a possible oversight on our part, we should search for the answer; perhaps the artist is too much involved with a uniquely personal vision of the scene, a style traceable to his experience while studying in Düsseldorf. There is a predictable quality in his pictures, particularly so if we view only the large panoramic canvases. That there is more for us to discover becomes apparent as numbers of pictures, especially earlier studies for the large paintings, are brought together. A broader vision of his work becomes evident when groups of pictures are seen.

To Gordon Hendricks we are indebted for revealing these relationships, and for his guidance in planning the exhibit as well as preparing the manuscript for the present gallery book and for a larger manuscript documenting the artist's life and works, *Albert Bierstadt* (New York: Harry N. Abrams, Inc., 1972). Peter H. Hassrick, Curator, and Frances M. Gupton, Registrar, of the Amon Carter Museum, have organized details of loans and arrangements for the travel schedule to the five participating museums. To the directors of these institutions we are indebted for recommendations and aid in arranging loans, and particularly to Lloyd Goodrich, former director of the Whitney Museum, and Rudolf G. Wunderlich for their valued suggestions and assistance.

In a loan exhibit of such size as the present Bierstadt show, it is inevitable that we have many more obligations to individuals and museums than we can properly acknowledge. Special mention must be made of the generous aid from the Trustees of the Museum of Fine Arts, Boston, who have permitted seven canvases from their fine collection of Bierstadt works to travel in the exhibition. We are grateful to the professional staffs of the many museums who have cooperated with us in locating examples of the artist's work and arranging for loans.

Mitchell A. Wilder

Fort Worth
January, 1972

1. *Photograph of Albert Bierstadt, ca. 1872*
   Courtesy of Rosalie Randall Rooks, New London, Connecticut.

Albert Bierstadt painted his first important Western landscape in 1860. It had been thirty-five years since Thomas Cole took his celebrated trip up the Hudson River and came back with the three Catskill landscapes that launched the Hudson River School. And ten years had passed since Asher Durand painted his famous apotheosis, *Kindred Spirits*. There had been significant American landscapes before Cole, and Bierstadt was not the only Hudson River painter after Durand. But Cole had popularized the vocation, and by the time Bierstadt came along to do his part, many others had made important contributions to the first native American school.

In 1860, with Bierstadt's *Wind River Country*, the wane began—for Eastern landscapes in particular—and artists felt the need for new vistas to be glorified. Bierstadt's 1859 trip into Wyoming exhilarated him, and he soon gave off his European bent. Now he began to apply the exacting oil techniques of his native Düsseldorf to the newly-found glories of the Rocky Mountains. The decade following 1860 was the era of his greatest success, both artistically and financially, and coincided with what most historians consider the near-extinction of the Hudson River School. Hudson River artists generally and Bierstadt himself—an extension of the movement—continued to paint American landscapes and many Americans continued to like them. But the crest of the wave had passed, and members of a European school quite different from that of Düsseldorf—the Barbizon—were coming to the fore.

Bierstadt, the Hudson River School whether or not, continued to produce American landscapes to the end of his long life in 1902. Sketches, studies, and finished works from the 1890s have come down to us, and although some are repetitive, others are as interesting and engaging as any the artist ever painted.

Bierstadt was not the greatest artist America has produced, but most of his work is attractive, and some of it is among the finest in American landscape art. He began his work with a European tradition of training well after most Hudson River artists had reached their separate apogees, and continued it through the far-away flowering of Impressionism. His life was a bridge from the romance of Cole to the realism of the Ashcan School, and his work a reflection of what many Americans, naive and sophisticated, liked in the last half of the nineteenth century. It is for this reason—to show the full range of his work and, by it, to help illuminate the taste of the American past—that this exhibition has been assembled.

Albert Bierstadt was born near Düsseldorf, Germany, on January 7, 1830, and was brought to New Bedford, Massachusetts, by his parents when he had just turned two (Nos. 1, 2 and 3). We know little of his childhood and adolescence at his parents' home at the corner of Acushnet and Mill streets (No. 95), but by 1850, when he was twenty, he had made his decision for an art career. In that year he offered to teach monochromatic painting to his fellow townsmen. In the following year he had begun to exhibit and make an occasional sale, and by 1853 had achieved enough local fame to inspire both his family and others to send him to Düsseldorf for three years' training in the ateliers there.

Bierstadt's reasons for choosing Düsseldorf were obvious: his mother's cousin, Johann Peter Hasenclever, was a painter and teacher there, and Düsseldorf was, at this point in history, the center of the newest and most popular of art schools. The "Düsseldorf School" had immediately descended from Peter von Cornelius, who had become director of the Düsseldorf Academy—as opposed to the "Düsseldorf School," a name given to the way art was taught in Düsseldorf—in 1821. He made various reforms, including a lessened stress on painting from casts and more from life, a new emphasis on landscape painting—which particularly appealed to Bierstadt, and a much closer relationship between students and teachers and amongst the students themselves. In 1839 a landscape painter was even given a professorship in the Academy, a revolutionary move for any art school of the time.

But it was not to the Academy in Düsseldorf that students from abroad turned in Bierstadt's time. They much preferred to study with the teacher of their choice in his own studio, as was the custom in Paris. And by the time Bierstadt arrived, the Academy's landscape teacher had gone off to start a school elsewhere. Bierstadt's intention, in any case, was to study with his famous cousin. But he arrived in Düsseldorf to find that Hasenclever had just died, so he turned to his fellow American, Worthington Whittredge, and to Emanuel Leutze.

Leutze, the celebrated painter of *Washington Crossing the Delaware,* is said to have remarked, "Here is another waif to be taken care of."[1] But Bierstadt was not so helpless. Whittredge, the Cincinnati artist who was already there, wrote about the young student from New Bedford in quite a different way:

> He soon proved that he was not likely to be a charge upon anybody. He refused to drink beer or wine, and if invited to dinner managed to get around all such

invitations in a polite way, especially if they looked in the least as if they required dinners to be given in return. He had no money to spend in that way and preferred to be thought unsociable rather than impoverish himself by giving costly dinners.[2]

Possibly in London, on his way from Liverpool to the Continent, the young artist had bought a sketch-book (No. 4), which was filled the next summer with numerous drawings, and what may be his first considerations of how he was going to sign his paintings: should it be "A. Bierstadt," "ABierstadt" with the initials in monogram, just "AB," and in script or printed letters? He finally decided on "ABierstadt" with the "A" and "B" in monogram for most of his pictures, but occasionally he used just "AB" and sometimes, although not often, "Albert Bierstadt."

The sketch-book is one of a type manufactured by G. Virtue of London, and was in wide use. It would certainly not have been improbable for the artist to have bought it in America, but it is a little easier to think he bought it on his way through England. It has fifteen leaves and thirty pages, and every page has been used—even the inside of the covers. Addresses of the people he met—including a professor at Union College in Schenectady—are inside the front cover and opposite the inside of the back cover. Pencil sketches, slight watercolors of landscapes or details of landscapes, and several detailed figures of peasant women are in the book. Many drawings have notations as to the colors the artist evidently wanted to remember for possible future use (although I have connected none directly with a known painting). Occasionally he would note where he was and when. For example, on an October 16 (1854?) he left Westphalia and it was a foggy day; on an August 15 (again 1854?) he was in Iserlohn, and it was rainy.

Continuously during the summers, and as weather permitted at other times of the year, the young artist tramped about the Düsseldorf environs and into many corners of Westphalia, filling his portfolio with oil sketches. When the weather was bad during the winters, he worked these sketches up into his first formal composition, bucolic landscapes, and the course of his art was set. One such German landscape, *A Quiet Valley* (No. 7), and a study made outside a church in Kassel are in the exhibition (*Study for "Sunshine and Shadow"*, No. 6). Seven years later, with the artist well on his way to fame and fortune, this Kassel study became the basis for one of his great early successes, *Sunshine and Shadow* (No. 32). On another of

8

32. *Sunshine and Shadow*
     Courtesy of the Argosy Gallery, New York, New York.

these excursions, possibly this time as far afield as the Austrian border, *Tyrol* (No. 5) may have been produced.

Whittredge described Bierstadt's working methods in his *Autobiography:*

> After working in my studio for a few months . . . he fitted up a paint box, stool and umbrella which he put with a few pieces of clothing into a large knapsack, and shouldering it one cold April morning, he started off to try his luck among the Westphalian peasants where he expected to work. He remained away without a word until late autumn when he returned loaded down with innumerable studies of all sorts. . . . It was a remarkable summer's work for anybody to do, and for one who had little or no instruction it was simply marvellous. He set to work in my studio immediately on large canvases composing and putting together parts of studies he had made, and worked with an industry which left no daylight to go to waste.[3]

As soon as a picture was painted, it was sent to New Bedford to be sold. "His pockets soon had money in them," Whittredge wrote. At the end of the first winter's work after the first summer's sketching, Bierstadt sent a picture to a Mrs. Hathaway, a member of a prominent New Bedford family, and wrote her: "In a few months I shall have some large pictures on the way, and I hope I shall find some purchasers for them in New Bedford." When the local newspaper reporter saw these new pictures, he thought the local citizens should be proud of Albert Bierstadt, "for he is a New Bedford boy, by education, if not by extraction, and we can safely predict for him a successful and distinguished future if he continues to improve as he has done."[4]

Leaving Düsseldorf early in the summer of 1856, the artist traveled with his friend Worthington Whittredge and others through Germany and Switzerland down to Italy, where he lived and worked for a year before returning home in the summer of 1857. During his stay in Italy, and possibly in Rome, he produced *Italian Costume Studies* (No. 8), part of a mass of materials he gathered for such later works as *The Arch of Octavia* (No. 10), which was called *Roman Fish Market* by the artist but was purified when it arrived at the Boston Atheneum. Sometime while in Rome, on an excursion southward, he came upon a vista near Olevano and left us an impression of the place, *Olevano* (No. 9).

The American artist Sanford R. Gifford had also been in Düsseldorf with Bierstadt and was now in Rome with him. In May of 1857 he and Bierstadt began their trips south. They first went to Naples, returned to Rome, and then went to Capri, where they stayed a month. A study in the Boston

Museum and a big *Marina Grande* in the Albright-Knox Gallery in Buffalo resulted from this stay. Ravello, Salerno, and Paestum visits followed, then the two parted company, with Bierstadt evidently staying a bit longer in Italy and returning to New Bedford via England.

He got back in August of 1857 and immediately began to work up his many European sketches into finished compositions. Among these was *The Arch of Octavia* (i.e., *Roman Fish Market*), which he sold to the Boston Atheneum. Before it got to the Atheneum, however, *The Arch of Octavia* was shown in New Bedford's first group show, organized by Bierstadt and containing also *The Old Mill* (No. 12), evidently inspired by a Westphalian scene. *The Old Mill* was bought by a New Bedford family and has remained in the family ever since.

There were a number of other European landscapes in the exhibition, mostly unidentified with known works by the artist. Although it was apparently not in existence by the time of the show, June, 1858, *Italian Landscape* (No. 25) likely came into being during these months. Only rarely did the artist return to his European themes after he had once seen the glories of the American West in the following summer.

Late in 1858 the artist produced his first historical painting, *Gosnold at Cuttyhunk, 1602* (No. 11). *The New Bedford Evening Standard* announced it on the first day of 1859 and reported that it had been painted for Thomas Nye, Jr., who owned Cuttyhunk, that site on the Elizabeth Islands upon which Bartholomew Gosnold, New Bedford's founder, first set foot. *Gosnold at Cuttyhunk, 1602* was later exhibited at the Boston Atheneum, and there the artist described it in the catalogue as depicting not Gosnold's first landing, but a visit of some time later, on a trading excursion with the Indians. Besides being Bierstadt's first known historical painting, a *genre* he tried often and with varying success, *Gosnold at Cuttyhunk, 1602* gives us our first glimpse of another favorite theme. At the left foreground the artist has painted the wild animals that inhabited the land now being violated by civilization. This freshness, this unravaged wilderness was close to Bierstadt's heart for the rest of his days.

But Cuttyhunk's imagined wilderness had little effect on the artist in comparison to what he felt when he first saw the American West in the summer of 1859. In April of that year he began a journey to the Wind River Mountains, and by the time he was ready to come back he had been so struck with the beauty of the American wilderness that for the rest of his life he

1. *Gosnold at Cuttyhunk, 1602*
   Courtesy of The Whaling Museum, New Bedford, Massachusetts (Gift of Miss Emma
   B. Hathaway).

was driven to try to put it on canvas. At his best, he succeeded beyond any of his contemporaries.

In the company of the Boston artist, F. S. Frost, and armed with a stereograph camera and an introduction from the Secretary of War to the commanders of the various military posts along the way, Bierstadt joined the wagon train of Colonel Frederick William Lander in St. Joseph, Missouri. He was soon off on the greatest adventure of his life. Following the Platte to its Fork, and then through Wyoming (then Nebraska Territory) along the Sweetwater and Wind rivers to South Pass, the artist and Frost, together with a man to tend the wagons and mules, left the Lander party to work their way back home by themselves. A visit was made to Fort Bridger, and there or nearby the famous scout was sketched (*Jim Bridger*, No. 19). Along the Platte itself, the Oakland Museum's *Ox* (No. 14) and the Saint Louis Museum's *Nooning on the Platte* (No. 23) may have come into existence. On the way back, at Fort Laramie, *Grizzly Bears* (No. 18) may have been produced.[5] Further east, early in September, the artist and his companions were in Wolf River, Kansas. Here they took photographs, and Bierstadt made studies for the Detroit Institute's *Wolf River, Kansas* (No. 17).

Back in New Bedford with many Indian artifacts, the nucleus of what was to become a large collection (*Quiver*, No. 13), the artist could scarcely wait to capture on canvas some of the magic of his summer's journey. Either then or in New York, to which he had moved by the end of the year, he produced *Thunderstorm in the Rocky Mountains* (No. 15), now in the Boston Museum of Fine Arts, a particularly felicitous effort. *Horse in the Wilderness* (No. 24), another delightful result of the artist's exhilaration over the Wind River country, may also have been painted at this time. It is also possible, incidentally, that it was painted *al fresco* at the site.

Early the next year, with his inspiration still fresh upon him, the artist painted two more Wind River works—*View from the Wind River Mountains, Wyoming* (No. 26) and *Wind River Country* (No. 27). *Wind River Country* was commissioned by Gardner Brewer. When it was completed the artist wrote Brewer about it: "In the distance is seen part of the Mountains called the Wind River Chain, prominent among which rises Fremont's Peak . . . along the River, Sweetwater its name, we find the willow, Aspen, Cottonwood, and Spruce . . . I have introduced into the foreground . . . a Grizzly bear, feeding on an antelope. . . ."[6] When I first saw this painting,

17. *The Wolf River, Kansas*
Courtesy of The Detroit Institute of Arts, Detroit, Michigan (Dexter M. Ferry, Jr., Fund).

24. *Horse in the Wilderness*
   Courtesy of Mr. and Mrs. Lloyd G. Wineland, Washington, D. C.

27. *Wind River Country*
    Courtesy of Mr. and Mrs. Britt Brown, Wichita, Kansas.

in 1964, the bear and the antelope had been painted out: evidently some-one had thought the subject too grisly.

At the Annual Exhibition of the National Academy of Design the same year, 1860, the artist showed a large painting he called *The Base of the Rocky Mountains, Laramie Peak*. When the Buffalo Fine Arts Academy was organized late in 1862, the artist gave it his big *Marina Grande*, and this new painting, *The Base of the Rocky Mountains, Laramie Peak*, was bought by the Buffalo group for part of the nucleus of its new permanent collection. But in 1922 it was loaned to a Buffalo high school, and by 1933 had dis-appeared without a trace—not even a photograph.

Another Wind River landscape, *Wasatch Mountains, Wind River Country, Wyoming* (No. 29), was painted in 1861. The artist could see the Wasatch Mountains looking southwest from near the Wind River—not, as he later wrote on the back of *View of the Wind River Mountains* in the Boston Museum of Fine Arts—looking northwest.

In the same year, in a curious experiment with historical *genre, The Brother's Burial*[7] (No. 30) came along. And the following year the artist dug out his study of the Kassel church of seven years before, incorporated it into a large composition, and presented *Sunshine and Shadow* to the public gaze. This picture gave the artist his greatest public acclaim to date. But this celebrity was shaded by a *chef d'oeuvre* which now began to gestate.

While at the base of the Wind River Mountains, and where the Colorado River becomes the Green and rises into lakes in what is now Sublette County, Wyoming, Bierstadt had met and observed many Shoshones in their natural habitat. He idealized a Shoshone encampment, placed it on the shores of a lake which never existed and within sight of a waterfall and a series of mountain peaks unknown in the Wind River country, and produced a *mélange* called *Sunset Light* (No. 28), now in the public library of his home town of New Bedford.

But whatever cavilling we may do about the authenticity of *Sunset Light*, it is a remarkable expression of an artist's love for the American wilderness. And, perhaps more significantly, it was the first concept of a work that was to bring the artist the greatest fame of his life, and a work which we think of today when we think of Bierstadt—The Metropolitan Museum's *The Rocky Mountains*. A recently discovered small sketch that may be the first idea for both *Sunset Light* and *The Rocky Mountains* is in the exhibition (No. 33) as well as the artist's study for the war horse blanket on a tripod

2. *Sioux Village near Fort Laramie*
   Courtesy of C. R. Smith, Washington, D. C.

of spears in the left foreground of *The Rocky Mountains* (No. 16). When an engraving of *The Rocky Mountains* was announced, this amulet was described as follows:

> Beyond . . . is raised the amulet or charm, being the embroidered blanket of a war horse, over which the medicine man has uttered his incantations, which keeps evil spirits away from the tribe, and is supposed to guard the village from all attacks of a supernatural nature.[8]

This study may also have been used for an earlier painting, *Sioux Village Near Fort Laramie* (No. 22).

The nation was now in the throes of the Civil War, and the artist's friends, both painters and writers, were eager to become involved—at a safe distance. Several were drafted, but like Bierstadt himself escaped service by paying the $300 exemption fee. Few enlisted. A number wanted to see the war at a closer hand than was afforded them in New York, so they got permission from various officers in charge to visit the Northern camps near Washington. Bierstadt got his permission along with the others, and out of these experiences resulted sketches for *Guerilla Warfare* in the Century Association in New York. Another Civil War subject, *The Bombardment of Fort Sumter* (No. 31), was done from imagination, fortified with information gleaned in talks with those familiar with the terrain, and maps of the site.

Bierstadt sent *The Rocky Mountains* to Boston shortly after he had completed it early in 1863. Then, with the western wilderness calling him back, he set out again—this time for the golden shores of California. With him this time was the writer Fitz Hugh Ludlow (No. 20), who was to write an account of their travels for *The Atlantic Monthly*. Ludlow published a full account of these travels in book form in 1870, *The Heart of the Continent* (No. 55), for which Bierstadt made many sketches.

The two set out from Atchison, Kansas. After many adventures with buffalo hunting and painting (from which *Buffalo*, No. 38, may have resulted), an introduction to Brigham Young and an engagement with Goshoot Indians, the travelers arrived at the crystal waters of Lake Tahoe.

Soon they were in San Francisco, where they were wined and dined, and where *Cloud Study, San Francisco* (No. 36) may have come into existence. Here they picked up several others for a visit to the newly-discovered Yosemite Valley.

Outside the Valley, in a grove of giant trees, they paused for the hospitality of Galen Clark, the Yosemite pioneer, and Bierstadt made studies for a later Big Tree painting, with Clark at the base of the tree, *Giant Sequoia* (No. 72). In Yosemite the artist made studies for some of his most attractive, inspired works. In one undated painting, which may be from this time, he shows an artist sketching on the Valley floor, *Yosemite Valley* (No. 37).

Leaving the Bay area for a trip to Mount Shasta and Oregon, Bierstadt and Ludlow camped in the country north of Red Bluff, and *A Rest on the Ride* (No. 34) may be a memory of this episode. But "they burned to see the giant Shasta," Ludlow wrote, "and grew thirsty for the eternal snows of the Cascade Peaks farther north."[9]

When they got to the base of Shasta, they found settlers from Illinois named Sisson in a two-story ranch house in Strawberry Valley. Ludlow—and presumably Bierstadt—was enchanted:

> No family whom we encountered lived in such wholesome and homelike luxury as Sisson's. . . . Cream flowed in upon us like a river; potatoes were stewed in it; it was the base of chicken-sauce; the sirupy baked pears . . . were drowned in it; and we took a glass of it with a magical shiny rusk for nine-o'clock supper, just to oil our joints before we relaxed them in innocent repose. Our rooms were ample, our beds luxurious, our surroundings the grandest within Nature's bestowal.

Leaving the Sissons, they traveled northward toward Oregon, "Bierstadt's color box the fuller by a score of Shasta studies taken under every possible variety of position, sky and time of day." When they got across the Oregon border, Ludlow became very ill with pneumonia, but was nursed back to health by Bierstadt, "the best friend I ever had." Farther along, on the majestic gateway through Western Oregon to the Columbia River, the artist made several studies of the Payallup River with Mount Rainier in the distance. One of these, *The Payallup River and Mount Rainier*[10] (No. 35), is in the exhibition. Several years later the artist painted two *Mount Hoods*, made from studies he produced up the river from Portland. One of these is unlocated, but the other, *Mount Hood* (No. 54), is in the Portland Museum.

Returning to New York late in the year, Bierstadt set about working his sketches up into a series of magnificent views of his trip to the Golden West. Among these was another *Yosemite Valley*[11] (No. 44), now in the

34. *A Rest on the Ride*
Courtesy of Dr. and Mrs. Cortez F. Enloe, Jr., Annapolis, Maryland.

Wadsworth Atheneum, and a large view of Mount Rainier with the Payallup River in the foreground, *Mount Rainier* (No. 40).

In April of 1865 the *Shenandoah*, a Confederate cruiser, burned several whalers in the Carolinas. The newspapers carried full accounts of the event, and Bierstadt may have been inspired to paint *The Rebel Cruiser "Shenandoah" Burning Whalers*. This is evidently the work now in the Shelburne Museum, Shelburne, Vermont. *Burning Ship* (No. 39) may have been an experiment in this theme.

In November of 1866 the artist married Fitz Hugh Ludlow's divorced wife Rosalie, and while they were courting he painted a large Colorado scene in her honor, *Storm in the Rocky Mountains*. The original is now lost, but a chromolithograph remains (No. 48). The artist named, in his program for the exhibition of *Storm*, the highest mountain in the picture after his *fiancée*. But most critics thought Mount Rosalie impossibly high. "The whole science of geology cries out against him," *Watson's Weekly Art Journal* commented, and went on to say:

> Away up, above the clouds, near the top of the picture, the observer will perceive two pyramidal shapes. By further consultation with the index-sheet, the observer will ascertain that these two things are the two "spurs" of Mount Rosalie. Now, let him work out a problem in arithmetic: The hills over which he looks, as we are told, are three thousand feet high; right over the hills tower huge masses of clouds which certainly carry the eye up to ten or twelve thousand feet higher; above these . . . the two "spurs"; what is the height of Mount Rosalie? Answer: approximately ten thousand miles or so. Impossible.[12]

It has been said the Bierstadt's Mount Rosalie is the present Mount Evans, the highest peak in the neighborhood, with the name "Rosalie" and "Mount Bierstadt" being given to nearby peaks.[13]

He ensconced Rosalie in a new house he had built in Irvington, New York, a short distance up the Hudson from New York City. At first he called it "Hawksrest," and then "Malkasten," after the artists' club in Düsseldorf. A stereograph of a "Malkasten" interior by the artist's brother Charles is owned by the artist's relatives (No. 43). The house was celebrated, and was the subject of a detailed article and an interesting engraving showing the artist himself sketching on the lawn (No. 77).

> There is a sincerity and beauty about some of our modern homes, which show us that the seven lamps of architecture have not been lighted in vain. . . . The beautiful and peculiar villa of Mr. Bierstadt, on the Hudson, is indeed an

exponent of the improved spirit of the present age, when household art and household beauty have become household words. A large and substantial house, built of rough blue-stone gneiss, the granite of the Hudson, it rises on its lofty side-hill, crowned with towers, surrounded with galleries, and adorned with oriel-windows; it is at once picturesque, unusual, and sincere . . .[14]

Perhaps from the lawn, in front of the house, looking across the Hudson, the artist made studies for one of the few Hudson River views by this Hudson River artist, *Sunset Glow* (No. 41), not to be confused with the New Bedford Public Library's *Sunset Glow*, which has nothing to do with it. Another painting in the exhibition, *"Malkasten" Lawn View* (No. 42), may be actually of the artist's lawn.

"Malkasten" was built of gneiss and wood. It was three stories high, with a tower rising another story above the Hudson, near Washington Irving's "Sunnyside." The *Home Journal's* reporter described Bierstadt's search for a site:

"Here," he mused, as he looked with a painter's eye upon the scene before him, "will I build my home: here, in the coming years, will I dream dreams and see visions—such dreams as poets dream and such visions as artists love to look upon: here will I watch, through the changing seasons, the sun rise and set, and mark the gathering mist, the flying clouds and the changing foliage. In the far off mountains I will find suggestions of grandeur, and in the river flowing at my feet ideas of grace and loveliness. . . ."

However much Bierstadt may have looked forward to the changing seasons when he built his house, it was not long before the big, draughty place was too uncomfortable for him during the winters, and he began to make a habit of staying in a cozy apartment at the Brevoort, or in his old familiar Tenth Street studio.

In 1867 Bierstadt finished his largest picture to date. This had been commissioned by Legrand Lockwood for his great new mansion in Norwalk, Connecticut. This was the immense *Domes of the Yosemite*, which is now in a delightful period setting that was virtually built for it, the St. Johnsbury Atheneum, St. Johnsbury, Vermont. Planning to take a trip to Europe, the artist painted a small version of his big *Domes* before it left his studio, so that he could take it to Europe and have a chromolithograph made from it. Both the small original oil and one of the chromos are on display (Nos. 45 and 46).

When the *Domes* was announced, one critic jeered: "The title of his

41. *Sunset Glow*
    Courtesy of the Philbrook Art Center, Tulsa, Oklahoma.

45. *Domes of the Yosemite*
   Courtesy of Miss Amelia Peabody, Boston, Massachusetts.

next picture will be 'All Outdoors.'" A number of observers were beginning to feel that the artist sometimes identified quality with quantity. He had been warned by *The Crayon* years before against making size an end in itself, and now many inveighed against what they thought had become a habit:

> Mr. Bierstadt seems to be under the delusion that the bigger the picture is the finer it is. . . . He has spread himself . . . over a bigger canvas than ever before. The result is a work almost entirely destitute of grandeur, although professing to portray a scene of which grandeur is the chief characteristic; a work . . . which we think must open the eyes of many to the common place character of this artist's production.[15]

The Times was not so harsh, but spoke disparagingly of the artist's ingrained Düsseldorf habits:

> The painting is executed in Bierstadt's usual manner—that is, the style of Düsseldorf—a style that can be learned as an apprentice learns a trade, and which no disciple of that school ever seems to be able to unlearn or forget. All the beauty of his pictures is on the surface, and is visible at first sight.[16]

The artist and his wife sailed for Europe on June 22, 1867, and although the public still thought he was the greatest among American artists, the critics continued their sarcasm. "Bierstadt has gone to Europe," one wrote. "It is to be hoped that while there he will learn to reform his style, and be taught that merit consists in quality rather than in quantity."[17]

In his two years in Europe the artist had studios in London, Paris and Rome. In one of these he produced another Yosemite view, *Sunset in the Yosemite Valley* (No. 49), possibly *The Coming Storm* (No. 50), and *The Buffalo Trail: The Impending Storm* (No. 51). *Storm in the Mountains* (No. 91), said to be a Swiss view, may also date from this European trip, but perhaps more likely from an 1895 trip.

In Europe the artist and his wife visited England, France, Germany, Switzerland, Austria, Italy, and Spain. In France the artist was presented at the court of Napoleon III and was awarded the Legion of Honor. In Rome he visited Liszt, and the aging abbé played for his party of only four. In Vienna they heard the three Strauss brothers "in an evening long to be remembered,"[18] according to Mrs. Bierstadt's sister, who was then traveling with them. In London on July 9, 1868, the artist gave a sumptuous banquet in honor of Henry Wadsworth Longfellow, who was in England to accept an honorary degree from Cambridge. Prime Minister William Gladstone himself was there, and in spite of the wishes of the guest of honor, nearly everyone made a speech. At the top of the elaborate souvenir menu was Bierstadt's new monogram, the same as the one on an 1872 letter to the Russian Consul General (No. 65).

In Paris Théophile Gautier himself praised the artist's *Storm in the Rocky Mountains,* and in London the President of the Royal Academy, Sir Francis Grant, did the same. It was, Sir Francis said, "one of the finest landscapes that adorn our walls."[19]

Back in America before the end of the summer of 1869, the artist and his wife visited brother Charles and sister Eliza in Niagara Falls, where they were making their homes. Now the exhibition's *Niagara Falls* (No. 52) may have come into being. Up the St. Lawrence and down into the White Mountains, the artist gathered sketches for *The Emerald Pool* now in the collection of Huntington Hartford. "I never had so difficult a picture to paint," he wrote, "but my artist friends think it my best picture and so do I."[20] *Rocks and Trees* (No. 53) may be one of the numerous sketches the artist made while in the White Mountains in the autumn of 1869.

The efforts that went into *The Emerald Pool* may have started the artist worrying. Was he really losing his powers? Was he really getting out of date as some were now saying? It may have been these concerns that prompted him to go again into the West that had not failed before to inspire him to greatness. In any case, in July of 1871 he and his wife started out again for California, this time over the newly-completed transcontinental railroad, for a two-and-a-half years' stay.

Early in this sojourn, with *The Emerald Pool* resplendent at Snow and Roos' gallery in San Francisco, the railroad king Collis P. Huntington commissioned a painting that would depict the Central Pacific summit, where the railroad reaches its highest passage over the Sierras, with fateful Donner Lake glistening below. The artist made numerous sketches for this work— perhaps working hard to convince himself he had not failed. While near the high pass *Lake Tahoe* (No. 57) may have been produced. And the completed work, *View of Donner Lake*[21] (No. 68) is in the exhibition.

Among the Mariposa Indians at the gate of Yosemite the artist was caught by the camera of Eadweard Muybridge, later to be called "the father of the motion picture," who this very year managed for the first time in history to stop the motion of a rapidly moving horse on a photographic plate.

68. *View of Donner Lake*
   Courtesy of The New-York Historical Society, New York, New York.

53. *Rocks and Trees*
Courtesy of Wildenstein and Company, Inc., New York, New York.

52. *Niagara Falls*
    Courtesy of Sewell C. Biggs, Middletown, Delaware.

96. *Sunrise, Yosemite Valley*
Courtesy of the Amon Carter Museum of Western Art, Fort Worth, Texas.

Muybridge published his stereograph with the title *Albert Bierstadt's Studio* (No. 58). *Indians in Council, California* (No. 59) was evidently produced within hours of the photograph.

In San Francisco the artist dashed off a delightful little study, *Overland Trail* (No. 56), reminiscent of his overland days and gave it to a friend. More of California's trees may have come in for attention in *Pioneers of the Woods* (No. 61). *The Emerald Pool*, meanwhile, had left Snow and Roos' and had found its way to Austria, where it earned for the artist a royal decoration.

Back in San Francisco from a jaunt into King's River country, the artist learned that he had been given the Russian Order of St. Stanislaus in recognition of his services in seeing to it that the Grand Duke Alexis had had a good time when he visited America the previous fall (No. 62). His acknowledgment to the Russian Consul General, on a letterhead of his own design, is in the Henry Francis du Pont Winterthur Museum (Nos. 65 and 66):

> . . . I have just returned from the mountains and find an agreeable surprise awaiting me in the form of a letter from your Ambassador. . . . Please be kind enough to send me whatever you may have by Wells Fargo & Co. Express. . . .

In San Francisco atop Clay Street Hill, the artist had built himself a studio:

> This house, with its windows opening in every quarter, commands a magnificent view of the city below, and of the Bay, from the Golden Gate in the west to Mount Diablo in the east, including the whole sweep of its varied shore lines and studding islands. Here Mr. Bierstadt has been studying sunrise and sunset effects, in addition to finishing his *magnum opus* [i.e., *Donner Lake from the Summit*]. The large window—as big as the side of the house—which gives him the north light painters always want, commands at one glance a view of the whole passage from the Pacific Ocean to the inner Bay . . . a distance of six or seven miles. The light from the other and smaller windows is shut off with curtains when not desired.[22]

The last summer in California, and just back from the country near Mount Whitney, the artist wrote Josiah D. Whitney, the famous geologist then at Yale, his congratulations: "The highest and finest mountain in the United States has been named after you . . . a sort of corner stone to the edifice of fame erected for yourself in the world of science." (No. 69).

58. *Photograph of Eadweard Muybridge stereograph, "Albert Bierstadt's Studio"*
Courtesy of the California Historical Society, San Francisco, California.

59. *Indians in Council, California*
Courtesy of the Kennedy Galleries, Inc., New York, New York.

71. *Mount Whitney*
   Courtesy of the Rockwell Foundation, Corning, New York.

Now he and his wife boarded the train for home. Back in New York the artist painted three more scenes full of California memories. One was the Big Tree picture with Galen Clark, *Giant Sequoia* (No. 72); another was his version of what Whitney's namesake looked like, *Mount Whitney* (No. 71); and a third he called *Sacramento Valley in Spring* (No. 70).

He gave *Sacramento Valley in Spring* to the newly-formed Montreal Art Association, from which it passed to the present Montreal Museum and, in 1945, to a dealer and thence to the California Palace of the Legion of Honor. The Montreal gift was also a compliment to the Bierstadts' friend, Frederick Dufferin, Canada's governor-general.

The Dufferins gave a great ball in 1876, and the Bierstadts, resplendent in specially-tailored costumes, were at the center of the festivities (Nos. 73 and 74). Later the artist's friend the Marquis of Lorne, later Duke of Argyll and son-in-law of Queen Victoria, became governor-general, and during one of the visits to Canada *The St. Lawrence River from the Citadel, Quebec* (No. 79) came into being. An album of Canadian memories was kept by the artist and his wife, and that memento, with oil-painting covers framed in silver, has been preserved (No. 75).

Moose hunting with Lorne or Dufferin near the border in eastern Canada, possibly about 1880, the artist produced one of the exhibition's surprises, *Hunters* (No. 78). The palette is quite unconventional for Bierstadt: it is almost as if he had painted the picture in the semi-darkness which is depicted.

Bierstadt was a prominent member of the famous Boone and Crockett Club founded by, among others, Theodore Roosevelt. In approximately the same year as *Hunters* the artist bagged one of the largest moose ever taken in America. This was near the Canadian border, either in Maine or in Canada—the spot is disputed. In any case, the artist gave his moose head to the American Museum of Natural History, which, in turn, gave it to the Boston Natural History Museum. In the Boston museum it may still be seen atop another moose hide in the museum's great central diorama. The Boone and Crockett Club, at least on paper, set rigid restrictions on how its members must take their game. But the eagerness and regularity with which the artist hunted suggests that he was interested in the pursuit itself, along with his usual impulse to associate with persons of economic and social distinction.

79. *The St. Lawrence River from the Citadel, Quebec*
   Courtesy of the Boston Museum of Fine Arts, Boston, Massachusetts.

Around 1880 Mrs. Bierstadt's health had begun to fail. She had been delicate—and self-indulgent, if we are to believe her sister—for some years. But now she became so ailing that it was thought she should have a warmer climate. (Her ailment turned out to be consumption, for which, in the nineteenth century, a warm climate was the specific.) So the Bierstadts decided to make Nassau a resort, and for many years, with fair regularity until Mrs. Bierstadt's death in 1893 they took trips to this British possession, usually together, but occasionally the wife alone. In Nassau, as generally elsewhere, they involved themselves in the highest available social life, this time being entertained by and entertaining the various Nassau governors and their courts. Bierstadt was a courtly, kindly and congenial man, and his wife was thought to be beautiful and charming. As a result—apart from the artist's celebrity—they were much sought after socially.

Bierstadt made a number of pictures of his Nassau days. One of these, *Nassau Harbor* (No. 76), caught a steamer in the harbor.

In 1886 the artist traveled to Wisconsin, painting The Dells and the Lake Superior region. He sketched and sailed along the lake shore and among the islands north of Duluth, producing landscapes such as *On Lake Superior—Sand Island* (No. 82). On the way through Minneapolis he evidently stopped to visit friends, and painted, possibly, his hostess and her son in the library of their home, *Interior* (No. 81).

By now the dissent against Bierstadt's style of painting had swelled to a chorus. A California scene, *The Art Amateur* commented, was an example "of the dreadful things which were considered good art less than a generation ago."[23] Eagerly the artist sought acceptance amongst highly-placed friends abroad. He sent *The Wave* (No. 80) in 1887, and for a while he thought that perhaps the Duke of Sutherland would buy it. But even the praises of his friend Lorne, now the Duke of Argyll, who said the water was so inviting it made him want to "take a header"[24] into it, failed to effect a sale.

In preparation for the Paris Exposition of 1889, for which many American artists put their best foot forward, Bierstadt conceived a large, complex work, *The Last of the Buffalo* (No. 86). To him it evidently represented an apotheosis and a coda to his Western work. But in spite of formidable outcries to the contrary, ranging from the masthead of *The New York World* to the genteel protestations of Elizabeth Gardner Bougereau, the American selection committee turned down *The Last of the Buffalo*.

86. *The Last of the Buffalo*
   Courtesy of the Corcoran Gallery of Art, Washington, D. C. (Gift of Mrs. Albert
   Bierstadt).

The Committee of seventeen distinguished artists [*The World* editorialized sarcastically] who were appointed to select pictures for the American exhibit at the Paris Exposition paid a high compliment to Mr. Albert Bierstadt by rejecting his superb canvas, "The Last of the Buffalo." It is to Mr. Bierstadt's great credit that the vote in the negative was unanimous. Those who have seen the collection forwarded by this eminent gallery can best appreciate the delicate tribute paid to the artist in question. . . . What manner of pigmies of pigment are these alleged artists who are seeking a notoriety beyond the reach of their daubs by forming "committees" from their precious selves and then giving wide publication to the fact that they have "rejected" one of Albert Bierstadt's pictures?[25]

Bierstadt himself said he was "indifferent" to the rejection, but it is hard to believe him. He had "endeavoured to show the buffalo in all his aspects and depict the cruel slaughter of a noble animal now almost extinct,"[26] and was sorry that the committee did not see it his way.

In the summer of 1889, with the Paris humiliation enshrouding him, the artist took another trip. This time he went through Canada via the newly-completed Canadian Pacific Railroad. A large oil in the New Bedford Public Library, *Mount Sir Donald*, is a tribute to the entrepreneur who put the railroad through. Near Lake Louise the artist may have painted one of the freshest views of snow-capped mountains of his career, *Rocky Mountains, Colorado* [*sic*][27] (No. 89). From the same time, or possibly earlier, may have come another snowy mountain view, *Yosemite Valley, Twin Peaks* [*sic*] (No. 87).

Traveling onward to Vancouver, the artist embarked on the ill-fated "Ancon" for a coast-wise trip to Alaska. Off Revillagigedo Island the "Ancon" was wrecked, and while she lay on her side in the bay the artist captured the blue and gray Alaskan light in a remarkable way, *Wreck of the Ancon in Loring Bay, Alaska* (No. 88). The "Ancon" was backing off the wharf at three o'clock in the morning when "an excited Chinese, seeing the line slack . . . cast the light off the wharf pile. Before another line could be passed ashore the Ancon was carried by the tide onto the reef. When the tide fell she broke her back."[28]

Trips to Europe and Nassau filled the next few years. Now the World's Columbian Exposition in Chicago in 1893 was in the offing, and Bierstadt resolved to try his hand at a monumental memorial to the landing of Columbus. He traveled to Spain, Portugal, and the West Indies—particularly San Salvador—for his research. There were three *Landings of Columbus* from his hand, and one of these, owned by the City of Plainfield, New

88. *Wreck of the "Ancon" in Loring Bay, Alaska*
    Courtesy of the Boston Museum of Fine Arts, Boston, Massachusetts.

Jersey, is in the exhibition (No. 90). Another is in the collection of the Newark Museum, and a third, the largest of all—and the largest painting the artist ever produced—was given by the artist as a wedding gift to his second wife, and by her, after his death, to the American Museum of Natural History, where it was destroyed by order of the director in March of 1960. It had been hung in the power plant where it had evidently been badly damaged.

In 1882 Bierstadt's house in Irvington had burned, and regularly he lived and worked in New York City at the Brevoort Hotel or at the elegant Van Rensselaer at 1271 Broadway. It was at the Van Rensselaer that he held many of his characteristic *soirées*. One such "New York afternoon" was another occasion for the distribution of his famous "Bierstadt butterflies":

> We women were so glad we *were* women that afternoon, [a reporter recalled] for Mr. Bierstadt presented each lady with a souvenir. This is how he made them. We all clustered about the table and he took out a palette, a knife and some large slips of cartridge paper. Two or three daubs of pigment on the paper, a quick fold, and holding it still folded against a pane of glass, he made two or three strokes of the wizard-like palette knife on the outside, and hey, presto! a wonderful Brazilian butterfly or moth, even with the veining on the wings complete! A pencil touch added the antennae, the artist's autograph was added to the corner, and now each of us owns a painting by Bierstadt.[29]

There are three "Bierstadt butterflies" in the exhibition, one fairly large, from a private collection, and two more casual ones from the Winterthur Museum (Nos. 83, 84, and 85).

The last known work by Bierstadt, also perhaps the only known watercolor from his hand since the sketches of the 1854 student days, was signed and dated February 22, 1901 (No. 92). Four other works, only vaguely dated during the artist's "middle period," are also in the exhibition: *Sunrise, Yosemite Valley* (No. 96), *Fiery Landscape* (No. 97), *Blue Clouds in the Rockies* (No. 98), and *The Conflagration* (No. 99).

Albert Bierstadt exhibited scarely at all during the last years of his life, and there were few public notices of either himself or his work. When he died on February 18, 1902, in his home at 322 Fifth Avenue, New York City, the world little noted his passing. *The New York Times* called him "one of the foremost landscape painters in this country";[30] *The Boston Evening Transcript* cited his principal works, his honors, and his "high reputation";[31] *The New Bedford Evening Standard* took pride in a native son who had made good, and reminded its public that "probably no other American artist has secured so large prices for his pictures"[32]—which was true.

Two weeks later *The London Outlook* put the artist in perspective:

> . . . [the artist has been] almost forgotten by people of the present generation. . . . Forty years ago Mr. Bierstadt was perhaps more popular and widely known among people at large than is any American painter of the present generation. The defects of his work are very obvious, and they have been felt so keenly that his work is probably now undervalued.[33]

Current Literature predicted that "the day will doubtless return when his achievements will be recognized as they seem not wholly to be now."[34] This exhibition, it is hoped, seventy years later, will help fulfill that prediction.

Gordon Hendricks
New York, August 2, 1971

NOTES

[1]Worthington Whittredge, *Autobiography,* in the Archives of American Art, New York, New York.

[2]*Ibid.*

[3]*Ibid.*

[4]*The New Bedford Daily Mercury,* August 4, 1855.

[5]It has been said that the animals pictured in *Grizzly Bears* are actually American black bears.

[6]From a letter of February 10, 1860, in the Massachusetts Historical Society, Boston, Massachusetts.

[7]Or *The Brothers' Burial?*

[8]Quotation from a flyer announcing the publication plans for the print. Author's collection.

[9]This and the following quotations are from Ludlow's account of the trip in *The Atlantic Monthly,* July, 1864.

[10]This has been called Mount Hood, but the peak is clearly Rainier. It is the same peak as in the Union League's painting of the same locale, which for many years has been incorrectly called Mount Shasta.

[11]Not to be confused with *In the Yosemite Valley* in the same museum.

[12]The *Watson's* quotes are from the issue of March 3, 1866.

[13]These attributions, which I have not verified—Bierstadt's mountain profiles being so lyrical, are by John L. J. Hart, *Fourteen Thousand Feet* (Denver: Colorado Mountain Club, 1931). pp. 12-15.

[14]Martha J. Lamb, *The Homes of America* (New York: D. Appleton and Company, 1879), p. 149.

[15]*The New York Daily Tribune,* May 11, 1867.

[16]*The New York Times,* May 2, 1867.

[17]*Watson's Weekly Art Journal,* volume for 1867, p. 167.

[18]From a manuscript notebook of reminiscences by Esther Osborne, in a private collection in New York.

[19]From a May 3, 1869, clipping in a private collection in New York.

[20]Letter of June 5, 1870, Miscellaneous Manuscript Collection, Manuscript Division of the Library of Congress.

[21]Called by the artist *Donner Lake from the Summit.*

[22]*The San Francisco Bulletin,* January 11, 1873.

[23]*The Art Amateur,* January, 1888.

[24]From a letter evidently of May 5, 1887, in a private collection in New London, Connecticut.

[25]*The New York World,* March 31, 1889.

[26]Undated, but March, 1889, clipping from *The New York World,* in a clippings album in a private collection in New York.

[27]This title seems arbitrary to me. The only time Bierstadt saw snow capped mountains in the Colorado Rockies was while he was painting his picture for the Earl of Dunraven in 1876-77, *Long's Peak, Estes Park. Rocky Mountains, Colorado* seems to belong to a later period. It is very like a *Lake Louise* in a private collection in New York.

[28]Will Lawson, *Pacific Steamers* (Glasgow: Brown, Son & Ferguson, Ltd., 1927), p. 199.

[29]*The Detroit Free Press,* May 15, 1892.

[30]*The New York Times,* February 19, 1902.

[31]*The Boston Evening Transcript,* February 18, 1902.

[32]*The New Bedford Evening Standard,* February 19, 1902.

[33]*The London Outlook,* March 1, 1902.

[34]*Current Literature,* April, 1902.

CHECK LIST

1. *Photograph of Albert Bierstadt.* ca. 1872. Lent by Esther Randall Bascom, Waterford, Connecticut; Rosalie Randall Rooks, New London, Connecticut; Joyce Randall Edwards, Dobbs Ferry, New York; Pauline Randall Perry, Jamesville, New York.

2. *Photograph after a daguerreotype of Christina Bierstadt, the artist's mother* by Peter Fales, New Bedford, Massachusetts (?). ca. 1851. Lent by Mr. and Mrs. Albert M. Turner, Orono, Maine.

3. *Photograph after a daguerreotype of Henry Bierstadt, the artist's father* by Peter Fales, New Bedford, Massachusetts (?). ca. 1851. Lent by Mr. and Mrs. Albert M. Turner, Orono, Maine.

4. *Bierstadt's European Sketchbook.* 1854. 4⅜″ x 8″. Lent by the Addison Gallery of American Art, Phillips Academy, Andover, Massachusetts.

5. *Tyrol.* 1855(?). Oil on composition board. 13½″ x 19″. Lent by the Rockwell Foundation, Corning, New York.

6. *Sunshine and Shadow* (Study for No. 32). 1855. Oil on canvas. 19″ x 13″. Lent by The Newark Museum, Newark, New Jersey.

7. *A Quiet Valley.* 1855. Oil on canvas. 33½″ x 42½″. Lent by the Virginia Museum of Fine Arts, Richmond, Virginia.

8. *Italian Costume Studies.* 1856-57. Oil on paper. 11¼″ x 18″. Lent by the Lyman Allyn Museum, New London, Connecticut.

9. *Olevano.* 1856-57. Oil on canvas mounted on panel. 19¼″ x 26½″. Lent by the St. Louis Art Museum, St. Louis, Missouri (Eliza McMillan Fund). This painting is to be exhibited in two of the five participating institutions, the Amon Carter Museum and the Whitney Museum of American Art.

10. *Arch of Octavia (Roman Fish Market).* 1858. Oil on canvas. 28½″ x 37″. Lent by the Boston Museum of Fine Arts on deposit from the Library of the Boston Atheneum, Boston, Massachusetts.

11. *Gosnold at Cuttyhunk, 1602.* 1858. Oil on canvas. 28″ x 49″. Lent by The Whaling Museum, New Bedford, Massachusetts (Gift of Miss Emma B. Hathaway). The artist titled this picture, *Bartholomew Gosnold at the Elizabeth Islands, June 1602.*

12. *The Old Mill.* 1858. Oil on canvas. 43″ x 37″. Lent by Townsend U. Weekes, Oyster Bay, New York.

13. *Indian Quiver.* 1859 (date evidently acquired by Bierstadt). Lent by The Whaling Museum, New Bedford, Massachusetts (Gift of Miss Emma B. Hathaway).

14. *Ox.* 1859(?). Oil on cardboard. 11½″ x 18¼″. Lent by The Oakland Museum, Oakland, California (The Kahn Collection).

15. *Thunderstorm in the Rocky Mountains.* 1859. Oil on canvas. 19″ x 29″. Lent by the Boston Museum of Fine Arts, Boston, Massachusetts.

16. *Indian Amulet.* 1859. Oil on paper. 5″ x 4⅜″. Lent by Gordon Hendricks, New York, New York. (This was used as a study for The Metropolitan Museum of Art's *The Rocky Mountains* and for *Sioux Village near Fort Laramie,* No. 22.)

17. *The Wolf River, Kansas.* 1859(?). Oil on canvas 48¼″ x 38¼″. Lent by The Detroit Institute of Arts, Detroit, Michigan (Dexter M. Ferry, Jr., Fund).

18. *Grizzly Bears.* 1859(?). Oil on paper. 14″ x 16″. Lent by the Milwaukee Art Center, Milwaukee, Wisconsin (Layton Art Gallery Collection). The painting actually depicts American black bears, but in Bierstadt's day almost all bears were referred to as grizzlies.

19. *Jim Bridger.* 1859. Oil on composition board. 10″ x 7″. Lent by the National Cowboy Hall of Fame, Oklahoma City, Oklahoma.

20. *Photograph of Fitz Hugh Ludlow.* 1859(?). Lent by Alumni Association, Union College, Schenectady, New York.

21. *On the Sweetwater Near the Devil's Gate . . . Nebraska.* 1859. Oil on canvas. 12¼″ x 18″. Lent by National Academy of Design, New York, New York.

22. *Sioux Village Near Fort Laramie.* 1859. Oil on canvas. 13″ x 20″. Lent by C. R. Smith, Washington, D. C.

23. *Nooning on the Platte.* 1859(?). Oil on paper mounted on canvas. 6¾″ x 12⅞″. Lent by the St. Louis, Art Museum, St. Louis, Missouri (Gift of J. Lionberger Davis). This painting is to be exhibited in two of the five participating institutions, the Amon Carter Museum and the Whitney Museum of American Art.

24. *Horse in the Wilderness.* 1859-60(?). Oil on

board. 14″ x 19½″. Lent by Mr. and Mrs. Lloyd G. Wineland, Washington, D. C.

25. *Italian Landscape.* 1860. Oil on canvas. 22″ x 36″. Lent by Mr. and Mrs. Morton Funger, Washington, D. C.

26. *View from the Wind River Mountains, Wyoming.* 1860. Oil on canvas. 30¼″ x 48¼″. Lent by the Boston Museum of Fine Arts, Boston, Massachusetts.

27. *Wind River Country.* 1860. Oil on canvas. 30″ x 42½″. Lent by Mr. and Mrs. Britt Brown, Wichita, Kansas.

28. *Sunset Light.* 1861. Oil on canvas. 38½″ x 59½″. Lent by the New Bedford Free Public Library, New Bedford, Massachusetts.

29. *Wasatch Mountains, Wind River Country, Wyoming.* 1861. Oil on canvas. 26½″ x 40½″. Lent by the New Britain Museum of American Art, New Britain, Connecticut (John Butler Talcott Fund).

30. *The Brother's Burial* (or *The Brothers' Burial).* 1861. Oil on canvas. 18″ x 32½″. Lent from the collection of George Walter Vincent and Belle Townsley Smith, Springfield, Massachusetts.

31. *The Bombardment of Fort Sumter.* 1862. Oil on canvas. 26″ x 68″. Lent from the collection of The Union League of Philadelphia, Philadelphia, Pennsylvania. This painting is to be shown in three of the five participating institutions, the Amon Carter Museum, the Whitney Museum of American Art, and the Pennsylvania Academy of the Fine Arts.

32. *Sunshine and Shadow.* 1862. Oil on canvas. 39″ x 33½″. Lent by the Argosy Gallery, New York, New York.

33. *Study for "The Rocky Mountains."* 1862(?). Oil on canvas. 7¼″ x 10″. Lent by Fred Rosenstock, Denver, Colorado.

34. *A Rest on the Ride.* 1863(?). Oil on canvas. 30″ x 50″. Lent by Dr. and Mrs. Cortez F. Enloe, Jr., Annapolis, Maryland.

35. *Payallup River and Mount Rainier.* 1863. Oil on paper. 13¾″ x 19″. Lent by Henry Melville Fuller, New York, New York.

36. *Cloud Study, San Francisco.* 1863(?) or 1871-73(?). Oil on board. 13″ x 19″. Lent by The Oakland Museum, Oakland, California (The William and Zelma Bowser Collection).

37. *Yosemite Valley.* 1863-plus. Oil on canvas. 35½″ x 58″. Lent by the Pioneer Museum and Haggin Galleries, Stockton, California (Louis Terah Haggin Collection).

38. *Buffalo.* 1863(?). Oil on canvas. 13″ x 18″. Lent by the Rockwell Foundation, Corning, New York.

39. *Burning Ship.* 1865(?). Oil on paper. 9¾″ x 13¾″. Lent by The Hudson River Museum, Yonkers, New York.

40. *Mount Rainier.* ca. 1865. Oil on canvas. 54″ x 84″. Lent by The Union League Club, New York, New York.

41. *Sunset Glow.* ca. 1866(?). Oil on canvas. 26″ x 36″. Lent by the Philbrook Art Center, Tulsa, Oklahoma.

42. *"Malkasten" Lawn View* (?) 1866-82(?). Oil on paper. 12⅞″ x 17½″. Lent by Wildenstein and Company, Inc., New York, New York.

43. *Photograph after Charles Bierstadt stereograph of "Malkasten" interior.* 1866-71(?). Lent by Mrs. Orville DeForest Edwards, Dobbs Ferry, New York.

44. *The Yosemite Valley.* 1867. Oil on canvas. 36″ x 50″. Lent by the Wadsworth Atheneum, Hartford, Connecticut (Gift of John J. Morgan).

45. *Domes of the Yosemite.* 1867. Oil on canvas. 21½″ x 33¼″. Lent by Miss Amelia Peabody, Boston, Massachusetts. This is a copy for the chromolithograph of the large *Domes* now in the St. Johnsbury Atheneum, St. Johnsbury, Vermont.

46. *Domes of the Yosemite.* ca. 1868. Chromolithograph. 21″ x 32″. Lent by the Amon Carter Museum of Western Art, Fort Worth, Texas.

47. *Photograph of large "Domes of the Yosemite" in the St. Johnsbury Atheneum.* Lent by the St. Johnsbury Atheneum, St. Johnsbury, Vermont.

48. *Storm in the Rocky Mountains.* ca. 1868. Chromolithograph. 21″ x 32″. Lent by the Amon Carter Museum of Western Art, Fort Worth, Texas.

49. *Sunset in the Yosemite Valley.* 1868. Oil on canvas. 35½″ x 51½″. Lent by the Pioneer Museum and Haggin Galleries, Stockton, California (Louis Terah Haggin Collection).

50. *The Coming Storm.* 1869. Oil on wood. 9½″ x 13″. Lent by the Addison Gallery of American Art, Phillips Academy, Andover, Massachusetts (Gift of Mrs. Leon Bascom).

51. *The Buffalo Trail: The Impending Storm.* 1869. Oil on canvas. 29½″ x 49½″. Lent by the Corcoran Gallery of Art, Washington, D. C. (Gift of Mr. and Mrs. Lansdell K. Christie).

52. *Niagara Falls.* 1869(?). Oil on canvas. 19″ x 27½″. Lent by Sewell C. Biggs, Middletown, Delaware.

53. *Rocks and Trees* (in the White Mountains?). 1869(?). Oil on paper. 5⅛″ x 7¼″. Lent by Wildenstein and Company, Inc., New York, New York.

54. *Mount Hood.* 1869. Oil on canvas. 36″ x 60″. Lent by the Portland Art Museum, Portland, Oregon.

55. *Fitz Hugh Ludlow's "The Heart of the Continent".* 1870. Lent by the Amon Carter Museum of Western Art, Fort Worth, Texas.

56. *The Overland Trail.* 1871 (?). Oil on paper. 7″ x 11″. Lent by the Biltmore Galleries, Los Angeles, California.

57. *Lake Tahoe* (?). 1871-72(?). Oil on composition board. 13″ x 19″. Lent by the Amon Carter Museum of Western Art, Fort Worth, Texas.

58. *Photograph of Eadweard Muybridge stereograph, "Albert Bierstadt's Studio".* 1872(?). Lent by the California Historical Society, San Francisco, California.

59. *Indians in Council, California.* 1872(?). Oil on canvas. 16″ x 20″. Lent by Kennedy Galleries, Inc., New York, New York.

60. *Rocky Mountains.* n.d. Oil on paper. 6¼″ x 10½″. Lent by Mr. and Mrs. William H. Bertsche, Great Falls, Montana.

61. *Pioneers of the Woods.* 1871-73(?). Oil on canvas. 19″ x 25¾″. Lent by the High Museum of Art, Atlanta, Georgia. (Gift of the Exposition Foundation). This printing is to be exhibited in two of the five participating institutions, the Amon Carter Museum and the Corcoran Gallery of Art.

62. The Order of Saint Stanislaus, Second Class (Russia). Lent by Mr. and Mrs. Albert M. Turner, Orono, Maine.

63. *Hetch-Hetchy Valley.* 1872-plus. Oil on canvas. 37″ x 58″. Lent by the Wadsworth Atheneum, Hartford, Connecticut (Bequest of Mrs. Theodore Lyman).

64. *Hetch-Hetchy Valley* (Study for No. 63). 1872(?). Oil on canvas. 16″ x 21½″. Lent by Muriel and Edward White, Mamaroneck, New York.

65. *The artist's letterhead.* 1872. Lent by the Henry Francis du Pont Winterthur Museum, Winterthur, Delaware (Joseph Downs Manuscript Collection, No. 69 x 53a). This is Bierstadt's own design, possibly created in 1868.

66. *The artist's letterhead (envelope).* 1872. Lent by the Henry Francis du Pont Winterthur Museum, Winterthur, Delaware (Joseph Downs Manuscript Collection, No. 69 x 53b).

67. *Indian Pony.* n.d. Oil on paper mounted on board. 10″ x 7″. Lent by Kennedy Galleries, Inc., New York, New York.

68. *View of Donner Lake.* 1873. Oil on canvas. 72″ x 120″. Lent by The New-York Historical Society, New York, New York. The artist's title for this work is *Donner Lake from the Summit.*

69. *Photograph of Bierstadt letter to J. D. Whitney.* 1873. Lent by Yale University Library, New Haven, Connecticut.

70. *Sacramento Valley in Spring.* 1875. Oil on canvas. 55″ x 85″. Lent by the California Palace of the Legion of Honor, San Francisco, California (Gift of Gordon Blanding).

71. *Mount Whitney.* ca. 1875. Oil on canvas. 68″ x 116″. Lent by the Rockwell Foundation, Corning, New York.

72. *Giant Sequoia.* 1875(?). Oil on canvas. 117″ x 50″. Lent anonymously. This painting is to be exhibited in the first three institutions on the exhibition circuit, the Amon Carter Museum, the Corcoran Gallery of Art, and the New Bedford Whaling Museum.

73. *Photograph of Bierstadt in costume for 1876 Ottawa ball.* 1876. Lent by Mrs. Orville DeForest Edwards, Dobbs Ferry, New York.

74. *Photograph of Mrs. Bierstadt in costume for 1876 Ottawa ball.* 1876. Lent by Mrs. Orville DeForest Edwards, Dobbs Ferry, New York.

75. *Album with Canadian (?) scenes as covers.* 1876-plus. Lent by Esther Randall Bascom, Waterford, Connecticut; Rosalie Randall Rooks, New London, Connecticut; Joyce Randall Edwards, Dobbs Ferry, New York; Pauline Randall Perry, Jamesville, New York.

76. *Nassau Harbor.* 1877-plus. Oil on panel. 15″ x 20″. Lent by the California Palace of the Legion of Honor, San Francisco, California (Mildred Anna Williams Collection).

77. *Martha Lamb, "The Homes of America," with description of "Malkasten".* 1879. Lent by the Amon Carter Museum of Western Art, Fort Worth, Texas.

78. *Hunters.* ca. 1880(?). Oil on paper. 13½″ x 19½″. Lent by Mrs. Isabella Grandin, Boston, Massachusetts.

79. *The St. Lawrence River from the Citadel, Quebec.* 1881(?). Oil on paper. 22″ x 30½″. Lent by the Boston Museum of Fine Arts, Boston, Massachusetts.

80. *The Wave.* 1887. Oil on canvas. 53″ x 83½″. Lent by the Pioneer Museum and Haggin Galleries, Stockton, California (Louis Terah Haggin Collection).
81. *Interior.* 1886. Oil on canvas. 19¾″ x 14½″. Lent by the Boston Museum of Fine Arts, Boston, Massachusetts.
82. *On Lake Superior—Sand Island.* 1886(?). Oil on canvas. 14″ x 19″. Lent by The Knoedler Gallery, New York, New York.
83. *Butterfly.* 1873-plus. Watercolor on paper. 6″ x 9″. Lent by Florence Lewison Gallery, New York, New York. The earliest date known for a "Bierstadt butterfly" is 1873.
84. *Butterfly.* 1873-plus. Watercolor on paper. 4¾″ x 8″. Lent by Henry Francis du Pont Winterthur Museum, Winterthur, Delaware (Joseph Downs Manuscript Collection, No. 64 x 39.7).
85. *Butterfly.* 1873-plus. Watercolor on paper. 4¾″ x 8″. Lent by Henry Francis du Pont Winterthur Museum, Winterthur, Delaware (Joseph Downs Manuscript Collection, No. 64 x 39.6).
86. *The Last of the Buffalo.* 1888. Oil on canvas. 71¼″ x 119¼″. Lent by the Corcoran Gallery of Art, Washington, D. C. (Gift of Mrs. Albert Bierstadt).
87. *Yosemite Valley, Twin Peaks* (Canadian Rockies?). 1889(?). Oil on paper. 8″ x 8⅜″. Lent anonymously.
88. *Wreck of the "Ancon" in Loring Bay, Alaska.* 1889. Oil on paper. 14″ x 19¾″. Lent by the Boston Museum of Fine Arts, Boston, Massachusetts.
89. *Rocky Mountains, Colorado* (Canadian Rockies?). 1889(?). Oil on paper. 13¾″ x 19½″. Lent by the Boston Museum of Fine Arts, Boston, Massachusetts.
90. *The Landing of Columbus.* 1893. Oil on canvas. 80″ x 120″. Lent by the City of Plainfield, County of Union, State of New Jersey.
91. *Storm in the Mountains.* ca. 1895(?). Oil on canvas. 38″ x 60″. Lent by the Boston Museum of Fine Arts, Boston, Massachusettts.
92. *Landscape Study.* 1901. Watercolor on paper. 5″ x 8″. Lent by Dr. and Mrs. Carl F. Rainone, Arlington, Texas.
93. *Photograph of the artist's studio.* 1902(?). Lent by the Vose Galleries, Boston, Massachusetts.
94. *Photograph of the artist's studio.* 1902(?). Lent by the Vose Galleries, Boston, Massachusetts.
95. *Photograph of the artist's New Bedford home.* Pre-1941. Lent by The Whaling Museum, New Bedford, Massachusetts.
96. *Sunrise, Yosemite Valley.* n.d. Oil on canvas. 36″ x 52″. Lent by the Amon Carter Museum of Western Art, Fort Worth, Texas.
97. *Fiery Landscape.* n.d. Oil on paper. 6″ x 12″. Lent by Mrs. Orville DeForest Edwards, Dobbs Ferry, New York.
98. *Blue Clouds in the Rockies.* n.d. Oil on paper. 14″ x 19″. Lent anonymously.
99. *The Conflagration.* n.d. Oil on paper. 11¼″ x 15⅛″. Lent by the Worcester Art Museum, Worcester, Massachusetts.
100. The artist's palette, lent by Mr. and Mrs. Albert M. Turner, Orono, Maine.
101. The artist's calling card, lent by the Henry Francis du Pont Winterthur Museum, Winterthur, Delaware (Joseph Downs Manuscript Collection, No. 64 x 39.11).
102. *Rainbow on Lake Jenny.* n.d. Oil on paper. 17¼″ x 21¼″. Lent by the Chase Manhattan Bank, New York, New York.
103. *Photograph of a print of Malkasten.* 1870s(?). Lent by Mrs. Orville DeForest Edwards, Dobbs Ferry, New York.
104. *Photograph of Eliza Bierstadt.* ca. 1864. Lent by the Henry Francis du Pont Winterthur Museum, Winterthur, Delaware (Joseph Downs Manuscript Collection, No. 64 x 39.1).
105. *Canadian Rockies.* 1889 (?). Oil on paper. 14″ x 19″. Lent from the collection of Dr. and Mrs. Franz Stenzel, Portland, Oregon.